MW01173792

B.N. Me Me Her It Age

Quotes, Poems and Thoughts

(First Edition)

Tianna Latoya Billa

Percia Natia Billa Illustrator

Her It Age Publishing 2023
Library of Congress Control Number: 2022910234

ISBN 979-8-218-01370-7

Dedications

To my mother

This book is dedicated to you mom. I saw your sacrifices and I saw your struggles. I remember, when I was younger, when you would feed me and not feed yourself. I was small, but I saw. I remember, when I was in high school, you would every two weeks handover your full paycheck to pay for my classes so that I could stay on track and graduate on time with my peers. I saw your sacrifices, I saw your struggles. Your sacrifices and struggles were not in vain and that's why this book is dedicated to you.

To my children

You three guys make me want to be better and do better so that I can lead you by example. You make me want to break social and financial and educational generational curses that our family line has been plagued with for many generations. And I'm going to put a stop to it now. Not by skips and hops but by leaps and bounds. And this is just the beginning. That's why this book is dedicated to you guys as well.

And a special thanks to my oldest daughter, Percia, for helping me to adorn this book with her beautiful artwork. May you continue to be the great artist that you are and more.

Special dedication

To my kindred spirit and my soulmate Glenn Bruce: You are my best friend, my human diary, my other half. You mean the world to me and I love you. You believed in me more than I believed in myself. You saw my light and wanted to make it shine brighter. You always said that you wanted me to win. I have learned so much from you over the years. I know that I am a better version of myself because I had you in my life. I simply can't imagine my life without having had you in it!

To everyone else

This book is dedicated to each and every one who may have ever seen the light in me and did anything to make it glow brighter. And, for those who tried to snuff out my light, thanks for making me a fighter.

Poem book preface

I remember the first poem that I've ever written. It was like it was just yesterday. It was so emotionally relieving and also very cathartic. I felt a sense of calm come over me as the words from my head to my pen to my pad became its own entity as the words were leaving me.

I was a young teen disgruntled about going to an unfamiliar place with unfamiliar people to an in-law family wedding with my mother and her husband. She didn't want me or maybe didn't trust me to stay home with my older aunt who lived with us. During the car trip, the sky, the clouds, the moon and the trees kept me company as I didn't want to keep company with those who were actually with me. So with all of the natural inspiration around me, I was inspired to write the poem "Virginia Moon" which is included in this book.

I also remember watching the movie that starred Janet Jackson called "Poetic Justice". Even though the movie was good, I was really mainly interested in the parts of the movie where it reenacted Maya Angelou's poems. During those times of the movie I concentrated especially on every word of the character played by Janet Jackson.

But before all said prior, I fell in love with the poem that was written by a character named "Pony Boy" from The author S.E. Hinton's book "The Outsiders"; where he told everyone "Stay Gold". It was a very pivotal moment for his character in the movie I believe.

So as you can tell poetry has been a part of my life for sometime and I'm glad that I'm finally able to share my poetry to inspire others as some of my favorite poets have inspired me throughout my life!

CONTENTS

*All quotes, poems and thoughts are in
no particular random order by
preference of the author.*

"START WHERE
YOU ARE.
USE WHAT
YOU HAVE.
DO WHAT YOU
CAN."

-Unknown

"USE WHAT GOD GAVE YOU.
THERE ARE MIRACLES INSIDE OF
YOU, JUST AS YOU ARE. DON'T
WAIT.
CREATE, CREATE, CREATE!"

-ANITA BAKER

TWITTER @IAMANITABAKER

B.N. Me Me "Her It Age" (Quotes, Poems and Thoughts)

Them: How are you doing?
Me: Good, working on great.

-B.N. Me Me

On a rainy day like this, I would love to cuddle up to a brand new hardcover novel with a mug full of green or black tea with honey and lemon. While the lights are dimmed and in the background the faint sound of Fur Elise by Beethoven plays. And a lit candle with the sensational relaxing scent of lavender to further calm my inner peace. All while the kids are safe and sound at a loving trusted relative's home, so I can be in total relaxation mode!! God be willing, someday soon.

-B.N. Me Me

A handsome man is like eye poetry, speaking to me in rhymes and riddles and taunts.

-B.N. Me Me

I will love you now, for always, for ever, for eternity.

-B. N. Me Me

Love is something best shown, not just said.

-B. N. Me Me

Too much bullshit, too little love and respect and too late to make things right.

-B. N. Me Me

Living in a world where you can't decode the written language is a lonely world...so embrace literacy.

-B.N. Me Me

Men will give you then guilt you to get you.

-B.N. Me Me

Stop falling in love...walk casually into it with an open clear discerning and vigilant mind.

-B.N. Me Me

It's okay to dream big...Just as long as you wake up and do it big!

-B.N. Me Me

My empaths...Don't let your overactive view of optimism block you from reality.

-B.N. Me Me

I'm not shy nor meek...bull-shit is just a language that I don't speak.

-B.N. Me Me

You must need a tampon because you're bleeding from the mouth. Only pussies talk to women that way, respect me.

-B.N. Me Me

The most dangerous lie is that which has a kernel of truth.

-B. N. Me Me

The question shouldn't be, "Why don't I want to be bothered with you anymore?"; It should be, "Why would I want to be bothered by you anymore?"

-B.N. Me Me

Oh you're a Narc, get set, let go!

-B.N. Me Me

Stop being Stupid, you're too Smart!

-B.N. Me Me

God: Be strong my daughter.
Me: I will Father.
(Being obedient)

-B. N. Me Me

Even though someone may be fighting you
with lies and deceit, fight back with honesty
and integrity because you always come out
on top. You will be the victor!!

-B. N. Me Me

I know not everybody appreciates my
smiles, because to them it signifies that I
have something going on better than
them...but I don't, so don't hate my
happiness...If you only knew what I've
smiled through, what I am currently smiling
through and what I'm going to smile
through. You'll appreciate my smiles better.

-B.N Me Me

Toxic people 101:
The everyday rigors of life are already stressful enough. Then to allow a person to purposefully and intentionally disturb your peace for their own amusement is non-sensible. Ladies and gentlemen do not allow such persons to penetrate your life, period.

-B.N. Me Me

Obligated love is poor.
Voluntary love is rich.
And I am filled with opulence!!

-B.N. Meme

In an obvious study done by "GeeDumbAssReally" University. It states that if you keep away from those who use and abuse you the likelihood of you being used and abused greatly decreases by more than 1000 percent on average... ingenious!!!!

-B.N. Me Me

It's a sad day when "courtship" turns into "courtshit" because one can't get out of their feelings and move on.

-B.N Me Me

There is not always just strength in numbers. In my singularity, I have great strength because I have a GREAT GOD!!

-B.N. Me Me

I have a character flaw. I think about how my decisions will affect another person before I act on them. And, if I believe that somehow my decision would negatively affect another, who may matter to me, I will most likely not do it. However, I have missed out on a lot of things in my life that may have given me joy because of that. No more, I shall learn to think of myself first. Thinking of yourself first isn't selfish and ironically I have learned that from a lot of selfish people.

-B.N. Me Me

Goal-getters, I know it's disheartening and frustrating when your own family and friends don't support you in your goals.
But you have to keep it moving. This is what I say.
"You can either be my fan or be a fan and blow off!! Because with or without you, I will succeed!!"
Don't let them have you lose any of your momentum, keep it moving forward.

-B.N. Me Me

I.D'ing someone's personality swiftly is very important. It helps keep toxic people out of your life, before they can poison it. So, work on your...
(I =intuitiveness + D =discernment)
Pray on it daily if you have to!! Just do it!!

-B.N. Me Me

Toxic people are..
Peace disturbers & chaos stirrers
Don't walk away, run away from those types
of people!!

-B.N. Me Me

When you are served small potatoes, make
big chips.

-B.N. Me Me

Did I sense disappointment at my joy?
How about discontentment with my
happiness?
Sullen sadness in my milestones. Scorned
looks and groans at my talents I honed.

-B. N. Me Me

Hey, what's that sound?
Oh, It's my own thoughts that now I can
hear after getting rid of all of the toxicity in
the air.

-B.N Me Me

I may be in my ketchup phase right now but when I mustard through I'm going to be the hottest dog in the pound.

-B.N. Me Me

It takes a village to raise children and just one villain to destroy them.

-B.N. Me Me

All I can do is live with integrity and speak the truth regularly!

-B.N. Me Me

Silence is an abuser's fuel. Stop gassing them up!

-B.N. Me Me

Soft truths are better than loud lies.

-B.N. Me Me

They say, you can do bad all by yourself. I say, you can do better alone. Perspective matters.

-B.N. Me Me

Falling in love keeps you tripping, while walking in love keeps you upright!

-B.N. Me Me

If a man truly loves you he will try to keep you in peace not in pieces.

-B.N. Me Me

There's nothing more satisfying as a parent than to see your children safely relaxing and enjoying a household and all of the amenities that God has allowed for you to provide for them. I just can't explain the satisfaction in that...priceless.

-B. N. Me Me

When people ask me how I am doing I always reply by saying good and reaching for great.

-B.N. Me Me

I'm too deep to step into your shallow waters.

-B.N. Me Me

Sometimes as a woman I wonder how I can make everyone else around me feel safe, loved and secure all while I'm feeling unsafe, unloved and insecure.

-B.N. Me Me

When you panic you sink. When you relax you float!

-B.N. Me Me

The more I learn to truly love myself, the more I learn to fall out of love with those who only pretended to love me.

-B.N. Me Me

I learned from pain, from which all my wisdom was gained.

-B.N. Me Me

I used to want a thug guy who could come into the house and tear it up!! But now I just want a nice guy who can fix all that shit up that he broke...like maybe a general contractor or something.

B.N. Me Me

When you think about it these apps are replacing a good man. Whenever I need a ride to run an errand I just call an "Uber". Whenever I need to go grocery shopping or need something from the pharmacy I just hit up "Instacart". And whenever I need something fixed in the house [just contact "thumbtack" and breeze through the contractors profiles. And whenever I need to get to sleep at night and I need some attention I just hit up B.O.B, my Battery Operated Boyfriend that I ordered from Amazon!!

-B. N. Me Me

Them: You must think I'm stupid!

Me: No, I never said that. I don't think you're smart enough to be stupid.

-B.N. Me Me

I have to stop worrying about things that I have no control over and start controlling the things that I do.

-B.N. Me Me

I ran your text that you sent me through Google Translate. And, the results came back and said, "This is bull-shit and it cannot be translated!"

-B.N. Me Me

If the truth shall set you free then there are some who must prefer bondage.

-B. N. Me Me

I am only fluent in the truth. I do not speak nor understand lies.

-B. N. Me Me

If you have given someone all that you got to give and you treated them better at times than you have even treated yourself; and they decide to turn their back on you and leave. The only thing that you can do is wish them well, watch them as they leave and move on.

-B. N. Me Me

Slow down sometimes and be in the moment, so that the moment can be in you.

-B.N. Me Me

What does music mean to me?

Music is cathartic, music is healing, music is the medicine to the soul, fuel for your spirit. Music is a universal language that everyone speaks the same worldwide...it has no communication boundaries. And I'm just so glad that God has entrusted me with this gift to give and share with the multitude.

So, please join me on this journey to breathe life into my intellectual properties that I put my pen to the pad and inserted passion to the pages to create!!

-Tianna Billa

www.TiannaBilla.com

I don't have trust issues, you have honesty issues.

-B.N. Me Me

I'd rather be by myself and happy then with a crowd and miserable.

B.N. Me Me

Never give someone your all, because when they walk away with it, you will be empty. Give them only as much as you can spare to still keep you full if they leave.

B. N. Me Me

I used to want a thug guy who could come into the house and tear it up!! But now I just want a nice guy who can fix all that shit up that he broke...like maybe a general contractor or something.

-B.N. Me Me

Flakes are only good in a bowl with milk.

-B.N. Me Me

DNA means nothing if you

Do

Not

Act

like family!!

-B.N. Me Me

Just like a very expensive rug, they may lie very well but ain't nobody buying it!

-B.N. Me Me

It's funny how the more you try to mind your own business the more others try to mind yours.

-B.N. Me Me

They painted the ugly picture of themselves, all I did was frame it.

-B.N. Me Me

Those who have a hot temper usually have a cold heart.

-B.N. Me Me

Do more and say less.

-B.N. Me Me

If you can't do Leaps and Bounds do Skips and Hops.

-B.N. Me Me

Lately, I have been so blue that denim envies me.

-B.N. Me Me

The silence is so loud. So I sleep with the TV on to try to mutter it until I can sleep without it again.

-B.N. Me Me

When they say "You look like you lost your best friend." Unfortunately, when I look in the mirror every morning, I know what that looks like now.

-B.N. Me Me

Those who say they have nothing against you, they have nothing to forward you either.

-B.N. Me Me

I don't expect everyone to like me. But I do expect for you to have a legitimate reason why you don't.

-B.N. Me Me

You ever put your stuff in a safe place only to find out that you've hidden it from yourself when you go to retrieve it later.

-B.N. Me Me

All song writers are poets, but not all poets are songwriters.

-B.N. Me Me

You make music because you love it. You get paid for it because others love it.

-B.N. Me Me

There are two types of people, those who hurt and hinder and those who heal and help. Spend more of your time with the latter.

-B.N. Me Me

Push forward or fall back. The choice is yours!

-B.N. Me Me

Plant seeds to grow trees.

Even though you may never eat of its fruit.

Plant seeds to grow trees.

Even though you may never rest in its shade.

Plant seeds to grow trees.

That may feed plenty and shade many.

But never may feed or shade you!

Plant seeds to grow trees

So that generation after generation can come to harvest.

Plant seeds to grow trees

So that they may keep generational wealth close in their pockets of their vest

Oh, let me further impress

upon those who don't believe in planting a seed and then I'll digress

This world, oh what would it be

As screwed up as it may now seem

Oh but ponder the thought on what would it be

If those before us did not plant a seed to grow a tree

For you and for me.

I beg of you, please plant a seed.

-B.N. Me Me

Temptation and curiosity is a bitch.

Just a little bit on my tongue I wanted to lick.

But then I devoured you up,

Damn what the fuck!

Temptation and curiosity is a bitch!!

-B.N. Me Me

Get rid of anyone in your life who does more hurting, harming and hindering then helping, healing and honoring.

-B.N. Me Me

Friendships are fleeting and family is fickle but God is forever!

-B.N. Me Me

Remember, no is not never.

-B.N. Me Me

They say, think like a boss. I say, do like a boss.

-B.N. Me Me

I believe in being in two places at one time, because while I was over the moon I was under you.

-B.N. Me Me

While no love may be lost, no respect is gained.

-B.N. Me Me

When you have been so selfless to a person that has only been selfish towards you, it's time to let go.

-B.N. Me Me

I come from meager soil to immerse into a beautiful flower.

-B.N. Me Me

Never feel foolish for defending someone even if they run right back to the very thing that you were defending them from. At least you know your intentions were pure

-B.N. Me Me

Stop throwing the word friend around so easily. Save the word for those who truly deserve it.

-B.N. Me Me

As I looked into the water, I had time to reflect on how deep my feelings were for you. Until I threw in a rock and it sank.

-B.N. Me Me

The ones you love the most can hurt you the most.

-B.N. Me Me

Even if you do everything right, it can still turn out wrong!
-B.N. Me Me

Either you are all in or you are not in at all.
-B.N. Me Me

Letting go is hard, but not letting go is harder.
-B.N. Me Me

You're not going to like everyone you love and you are not going to love everyone you like, and that's ok.
-B.N. Me Me

Don't let your failures defeat and define you, let your failures prep and design you.
-B.N. Me Me

Un-tilt your crown and flip that frown.

-B.N. Me Me

You Know you have a lot on your mind
when you are watching television on mute
and don't even realize it.

-B.N. Me Me

Ladies, don't forget to have some "YOU"
time...do your hair, your face, and your
nails...Self-care is not about being vain but
about being sane. Because, when you look
good on the outside you definitely feel better
on the inside!

-B. N. Me Me

April is national poetry month. So pick up
your pens my poets and put it to the paper!

-B. N. Me Me

APRIL IS NATIONAL POETRY MONTH!!

I want to make you my habit.

Pull you out my magic hat like you're a rabbit.

Turn you on and scroll you like you're my tablet.

Baby, be my habit.

Just thinking about you leaves me half wit.

Can't believe you got me smitten with this shit.

Don't need no 12 steps, just need your caress.

Count your heartbeats while I'm laying on your chest.

Baby, won't you be my habit.

Just say you'll be ecstatic.

Been itching for you like I'm an addict.

Just be my habit, just be my habit.

-B. N. Me Me

By trying to rescue someone who doesn't want to be rescued, you risk your own mortality.

-B. N. Me Me

It's better to be your own boss then get someone else rich by letting them be your boss.

-B. N. Me Me

A little hope is all you need to ignite this spark into a flame then into a full-blown fiery infernal.

-B. N. Me Me

The truth stings for a moment but deception bites for life.

-B. N. Me Me

If I gained the world, I would net the sky.

-B. N. Me Me

My blissful forbidden fruit, when I bit into you parts of you got stuck in my tooth. I licked at you with my tongue to get you loose, but ain't no use, but ain't no use.

-B. N. Me Me

Women, be about that boss-life. If a man has a "no-call no-show", just fire and rehire.

-B. N. Me Me

Note to self, I love you.

-B. N. Me Me

Loving and putting yourself first is not selfish, it's necessary.

-B. N. Me Me

The slight pause that you get is not for nothing; it's your mind's intuition telling you to give it another thought.

-B. N. Me Me

True freedom is when you can paint the town red or whatever fucking color you want!

-B. N. Me Me

You should really think about thinking sometimes.

-B. N. Me Me

Filter out the bad and focus on the good; for whatever you neglect will die and whatever you nourish will flourish.

-B. N. Me Me

They say what you don't know won't hurt. I say what you don't know could severely devastated, destroy and damage every portion of your life.

-B. N. Me Me

I'd rather you stab me in my back in front of my face, please.

-B. N. Me Me

Knowing your lineage is very important. I know who I am and I know whose I am. I am the royal daughter of the King of Kings, the Lord of Lords, the most high God.

Ladies know your worth. Would the daughter of a king take just any old kind of treatment from any old peasant on the street? I don't think so…know your worth!!

-B. N. Me Me

Never cry over spilt milk, or a serial liar.

-B. N. Me Me

Time is one valuable thing that we cannot accumulate in abundance, use it wisely!

-B. N. Me Me

Don't let the presentation fool you, pieces of cracked shells can ruin the whole omelet.

-B. N. Me Me

A shove in the back is tough love, a stab in the back is weak hate.

-B. N. Me Me

They say better said than done, I say better done than said.

-B. N. Me Me

Trust is lost in bricks, and gained back in granules.

-B. N. Me Me

I promise, I'll do everything that I can do to make you happy. And then I walked away from the mirror to begin my day.

-B.N. Me Me

Be aware of those who speak a lot yet have nothing to say.

-B.N. Me Me

When you feel like you have nothing to lose it's just at that very moment that you have all to gain.

-B.N. Me Me

I won't curse you out but I will pray you out! Because that's what real prayer warrior women do!

-B.N. Me Me

After dealing with toxic people you can gain back your sanity and heal your wounds; but you can't get back the time you lose.

-B.N. Me Me

Life is like a candy store. There are two kinds of candy, sweet and sour. Just make sure in life you ingest more of the sweet and less of the sour.

-B.N. Me Me

Intimacy is not always just about sex. Sometimes, I may just want you to hold me until I fall asleep on your chest.

-B.N. Me Me

I want to be free to love who I want, whenever I want, without anyone telling me that I can't.

-B.N. Me Me

I'm not cocky, just confident, I'm not snooty, just particular and I'm not a smart ass I'm just intelligent! And, I'm definitely not gullible because I'm damn sure not going for your bull-shit!

-B.N. Me Me

People lie on you because they know that there is nothing that they can say about you that is true that will make you look bad because you look so good!

-B.N. Me Me

I tell men that a mind is a terrible thing to waste if you are only concentrating on what's below my waist.

-B.N. Me Me

I love more than some and like less than many.

-B.N. Me Me

ID'ing someone is not about looking at their driver's license. It's about being intuitive and discerning about their character.

-B.N. Me Me

Learning to know someone from the inside out instead of from the outside in will save you a lot of time and grief.

-B.N. Me Me

Be aware of those who criticize more than they empathize.

-B.N. Me Me

No, it's not you, it's them. Please know that.

-B.N. Me Me

She was not prepared for half of what she went through but through God's grace she came out whole.

-B.N. Me Me

When given an ultimatum always choose you!

-B.N. Me Me

Better to be apart and happy than together and miserable.

-B.N. Me Me

A penny will eventually add up to be a dollar for as long as you are persistent and consistent even if it takes all of 100 tries.

-B.N. Me Me

Hope is having options, penetrate everyday.

-B.N. Me Me

Make progress towards your goals everyday no matter how small.

-B.N. Me Me

Keep close to those who pray and far from those who prey!

-B.N. Me Me

Weak person: I hurt so I want others to hurt too.

Strong person: I hurt, I would never wish this pain on another.

-B.N. Me Me

Never let anyone make you feel guilty for setting boundaries. If anyone is uncomfortable with the boundaries that you set in your life, it is their problem not yours.

-B.N. Me Me

Choose your friends wisely, since you can't choose your family.

-B.N. Me Me

It's better to eat alone in peace than to eat with many in chaos.

-B.N. Me Me

It's her heritage, it's her it age.

It's never too late to accept the love that God has given you, giving you.

It's her heritage, it's her it age, it's never too late to accept the legacy that God has blessed you, blessed you.

His timing is not our time.

His timing is oh so divine.

This feeling is also fine. Take it, cause it's your heritage.

-B.N. Me Me

Remember, your rainy days are here to make you blossom and grow.

-B.N. Me Me

In time doesn't justify staying with someone especially when they are just clocking you for control. Punch the "clock-in" elsewhere.

-B.N. Me Me

Your kindness may have been mistaken for your weakness but it is your strength.

-B.N. Me Me

Don't ever cease to be amazed because it keeps the light in you bright!

-B.N. Me Me

Researchers have just discovered that "No" is a complete thought, period.

-B.N. Me Me

You can hurt someone to pieces or you can love them whole.

-B.N. Me Me

Just say nope! My empaths, I know sometimes it's hard to say "No" but if you can't say "No" just say "N.O.P.E" (No to Obligations Passed on Expectations!

-B.N. Me Me

Those who don't dream, don't rest well!

-B.N. Me Me

Broken people can't give you whole pieces.

-B.N. Me Me

On my journey to becoming "G.R.E.A.T", I must G.et R.eally E.xcited A.bout T.oday first!

-B.N. Me Me

Creative people be E.QU.A.L

E.ccentric QU.uirky A.nd L.oving!

-B.N. Me Me

It's your imperfections that make you
perfect.

-B.N. Me Me

A cry for help does not always include tears.

-B.N. Me Me

Hating your Ex more than you love your
children is never okay, period.

-B.N. Me Me

It's better to be raised in a household with one whole parent than with two broken parents.

-B.N. Me Me

I will no longer be A. D.O.P.E for love!

(A.drenaline, D.opamine, O.xytocin, P.heromones, E.ndorphins)

-B.N. Me Me

It's better to wake up out of the clouds later, then to be caught in the thunderstorm forever.

-B.N. Me Me

I would rather know a little about a lot than a lot about a little.

-B.N. Me Me

If a tree bears bad fruit, then take an ax to the root.

-B.N. Me Me

Ladies and gentlemen get with a mate that compliments you, not completes you. You should be complete all on your own.

-B.N. Me Me

T.H.I.N.K

T.ake

H.eed

I.n

N.ewfound

K.nowledge

-B.N. Me Me

Who keeps the sun away just far enough so that it won't ignite us into flames? Who separates the massive oceans from the land, is it man? Who hangs the stars in the sky at night, just in the right spot so that we can see the 12 constellations in perfect formation all the way from Aries to Gemini, no sir, it is not I.

Who allowed the sperm in the womb so that it may turn into you. What makes the animals that are wild keep to their bounds? Who gives us dominion even though we are outweighed by the millions.

Who turns the world on its perfect tilted axis all the way 360° degrees around each day within 24 hours without letting us down. Oh, if I could just crown...Who's ever responsible for these types of things, I would definitely call him my Lord and be in awe while He reigns!

-B.N. Me Me

Enjoy where you are, until you get where you want.

-B.N. Me Me

Before you commit to breakfast, crack the egg to see if any shells fall into the joke. If it does, scramble quickly and beat it!

-B.N. Me Me

If you choose to play in the mud, you'll have no one to blame for your dirty laundry!

-B.N. Me Me

Sticks and stones may break my bones but names will permanently scar me!

-B.N. Me Me

Virginia Moon, I see you trying to hide behind the clouds and the trees but I still see. Although I'm far away from home, I'll never be alone. Because you follow me you assure me never once have you bored me.

-B.N. Me Me

If you see me struggling don't criticize me, help me!

-B.N. Me Me

You should never be abused simply for loving someone.

-B.N. Me Me

Life has you stressed?

I am not my GPA.

I am not my fico.

I am not my birth age.

I am not my bank account balance.

I am not my ZIP code.

I am not my social security number.

I am more than just a series of digits.

I am me, totally naturally plain ol' me!

-B.N. Me Me

Have you ever noticed that the only score that has been the most important until you hit the workspace is your GPA and after that all the way through the rest of your life it's your FICO. The transition is slightly unnoticeable but real. Are we all just numbers?

-B.N. Me Me

Toxic People Awareness Month.

January

February

March

April

May

June

July

August

September

October

November

December!!

-B.N. Me Me

There's a liar in the familiar, be aware!

-B.N. Me Me

Save your love for those who love you, not loathe you.

-B.N. Me Me

Be you, why?

Because,

Y.ou're

O.fficially

U.nique!

-B.N. Me Me

I can't work with anyone who is acting out of spite instead of out of what is right.

-B.N. Me Me

Being a victim of domestic violence is not shameful. Being the abuser in domestic violence is this shameful role.
-B.N. Me Me

Be happy, until you can be happy.

-B.N. Me Me

Haters, the energy that you are using to hold me back, you could be using to push yourself forward.

-B.N. Me Me

You bite the hand that feeds you and expect to be fed?

-B.N. Me Me

Shame on the person who deceived you, no shame on the person who believed you.

-B.N. Me Me

I'm a multifaceted woman who is rich with talent, gifted by God and driven by Passion!

-B.N. Me Me

Everyone knows a "whether" girl.
You know the woman that does what she needs to do, whether or not she has support. The woman who keeps her head up high, whether or not she has anyone to encourage her. And, the woman who keeps on going, whether or not she has anyone pushing her along to get it done. This whether girl does not get the glam and the attention of being on television but all she needs is the love and attention from her kids. The new whether girl, you can see her at work at a household near you!

-B. N. Me Me

Beware of those who are fast to take and slow to give.

-B.N. Me Me

I'd rather struggle in peace than be assisted in chaos.

-B.N. Me Me

These cynical, sadistic, vile, heinous, deviant, wicked and soulless creatures that walk the face of the earth to create chaos and kill peace. They disrupt, dismantle, destroy and damage anything that is good. Please, be aware of these creatures. They are called narcissists! Literally run for your very lives if you ever encounter one! And may God be with you if you ever do!

-B.N. Me Me

Your dreams should not be stored away in your subconscious. Not working to make them real and tangible is tragically obnoxious.

-B.N. Me Me

Domestic violence awareness. Domestic violence\abuse awareness. Isolation aggravates abuse. Silence deepens wounds. Avoid being isolated and avoid being silent. Tell anyone who will listen!

-B.N. Me Me

As much as I prayed for God to bless me with my kids, I pray even more now that I have them!!

-B.N. Me Me

I like having the last laugh. When people say I won't, I will. When people say I can't, I do. When people say fuck you, I say fuck you too!

-B.N. Me Me

I'm too lazy to be deceitful. I'd rather tell you the truth and get that shit over with, just saying.

-B.N. Me Me

Simply want to be in your presence. Hugging while inhaling your essence. All that sex shit can be saved for later. Ride me on your mental escalator. If your hair is long I will braid ya. Your love is real, I can see it in your behavior.

-B.N. Me Me

You are my king. If I had a magazine, you'd be on the cover of every issue. You love me so hard, you make me cry, I need a tissue!

-B.N. Me Me

There's always more than one way to skin a cat and I'm best at that. Block me here and I enter over there. Block me from the front and I enter from the rear. Lock the doors yet that's my specialty Houdini locksmith going to make a key. Pursue me my haters you ain't seen the best of!

-B.N. Me Me

I am your wonder woman

Your super wonder woman

I am your wonder woman

Wondering why you hang out all night

I wonder

Wondering why you keep picking fights

I wonder

Wondering why we can't get it right

I wonder

Wondering why I can't see the light

Inside of this dark tunnel

-B.N. Me Me

My circle is a triangle because I have to try different angles to see how I would get things done myself. But I don't mind because that just makes me three times on point.

-B.N. Me Me

Who digs in the dirt and then complains there's a hole there?

-B.N. Me Me

Jealousy is possessiveness. Possessiveness is ownership. And, ownership is slavery, think.

-B.N. Me Me

If my kids got paid for producing, developing, manufacturing, packaging, distributing, marketing and advertising EXCUSES, we'd all be filthy rich!

-B.N. Me Me

The Little Red Hen 2019

"Who will help me do the dishes?" said the Little Red Hen.

"Not I," said the first daughter.

"Not I," said the second daughter.

"Not I," said the son.

"Then I will just do it myself," said the Little Red Hen. And that's just what she did.

"Who will help me put out the trash?" said the Little Red Hen.

"Not I," said the first daughter.

"Not I," said the second daughter.

"Not I," said the son.

"Then I will just do it myself," said the Little Red Hen. And that's just what she did.

Who will help me spend some of this money from my direct deposit from work?

"I will," said the first daughter.

"I will," said the second daughter.

"I will," said the son.

"Oh, no the hell you won't! You ain't do your chores so you ain't getting a damn thing! I'll

spend it on myself!," said the Little Red
Hen. And that's just what she did.

-B. N. Me Me

Just because the man or woman does not
want anything to do with you. Your children
should have everything to do with you.
Don't make the children suffer for a breakup
that's not their fault.

-B.N. Me Me

"If you Give a Mom a Child Support Check" (Inspired by the poplar children's book "If you Give a Mouse a Cookie")

If you give a mom a child support check...she just may want to pay the gas bill with it. And when she pays that gas bill with it, she just may want to cook something for the kids. And as she is cooking something for the kids, she may need a different ingredient so she would take a trip to the market to get it. When she goes to the market to get it she receives a coupon for a trip to the zoo. So she takes the children to the zoo. As they are at the zoo, they may laugh and have fun! As they laugh and have fun, that may cause them to feel loved. As they feel loved it may cause their self esteems to become high. As their self esteem becomes high they may grow to become highly functional, independent, loving and caring parents themselves someday. So, be careful if you give a mom a child support check!!

-B.N. Me Me

Hey God,

I would like to order one daughter with dark curly hair, creative hands and a congenial personality. Another daughter with fluffy brown hair, precocious and inquisitive minded. And last but not least a handsome son, also with soft brown hair, quick witted and charming. Oh, and can you deliver them all seven years apart, I wouldn't want to over indulge! Thanks God, you're the BEST!

-B.N. Me Me

*For more information about the
author visit her website and her
social media pages.*

www.TiannaBilla.com

They say, think like a boss. I say, do like a boss!
-B.N. Me Me

Thank you Lord for keeping me from dangers seen and unseen Lord...I pray that you continue to be a fence around me and my family, Lord. I thank you for giving me peace even in the middle of chaos,Lord.....I thank you for making a way out of no way Lord, so many times...And for these things and many more I love you Lord with all my heart...In Jesus name...Amen.

FB post Nov 11, 2015 at 9:55 PM

www.TiannaBilla.com

IG: @BN_Me_Me

February 14, 2023

Made in the USA
Philadelphia, PA
February 14, 2023

ISBN 979-8-218-01370-7
51295>

Made in the USA
Columbia, SC
07 May 2024

34918989R00057